MARGARET
VISSER

MORE THAN MEETS
THE EYE

D0937949

PENGUIN BOOKS

PENGUIN BOOKS

Published by the Penguin Group. Penguin Books Ltd, 27 Wrights Lane, London
w8 5tz, England. Penguin Books USA Inc., 375 Hudson Street, New York,
New York 10014, USA. Penguin Books Australia Ltd, Ringwood, Victoria,
Australia. Penguin Books Canada Ltd, 10 Alcorn Avenue, Toronto, Ontario,
Canada m4v 3b2.Penguin Books (NZ) Ltd, 182–190 Wairau Road, Auckland 10,
New Zealand · Penguin Books Ltd, Registered Offices: Harmondsworth, Middle-
sex, England · First extract from *The Way We Are* by Margaret Visser, first
published in Canada by HarperCollins 1994 and in Great Britain by Viking 1995.
Copyright © Margaret Visser, 1994. Second extract from *Much Depends on
Dinner* by Margaret Visser, first published in Canada by McClelland and
Stewart, Toronto, 1986 and in Great Britain in Penguin Books 1989. Copyright
© Margaret Visser, 1986. This edition published 1996. All rights reserved · The
moral right of the author has been asserted · Typeset by Rowland Phototype-
setting Ltd, Bury St Edmunds, Suffolk. Printed in England by Clays Ltd,
St Ives plc · Except in the United States of America, this book is sold subject to
the condition that it shall not, by way of trade or otherwise, be lent, re-sold,
hired out, or otherwise circulated without the publisher's prior consent in any
form of binding or cover other than that in which it is published and without a
similar condition including this condition being imposed on the subsequent
purchaser · 10 9 8 7 6 5 4 3 2 1

CONTENTS

visserism ('visərizəm) *n.* **1.** a concise socio-anthropological insight arrived at by comparing current human behaviour with various alternative models, e.g., classical Graeco-Roman, Martian, etc. **2.** an entertainment in which points are made by identifying and skewering absurdities. **3.** any observation, esp. on contemporary manners, that provokes shocked laughter; a sly dig. **4.** *Archaic* or *literary*, the doctrine that all scholarship, e.g., food chemistry, etymology, particle physics, etc., exists to prove that life is rich, funny, and meaningful. [C20: from Anglo–South African–French *visser* to secure firmly or to screw in] – **visseriana** *noun* – **vissered** *adj.* – **visseral** *adj.*

Yes, But What Does It Mean?

Fresh off the boat from England in August 1964, we went into our first North American restaurant and ordered a hamburger. We had planned this event in advance – it was to be our first direct contact with the reality behind images we had known through movies, through television, through novels, through myth and fantasy, desire and suspicion and dread. We sat at a chrome-legged table with a red vinyl top, next to a smeary window. The waiter had come and gone, and had understood every word we said. It was very hot; enormous cars drifted past in the street. So far, so good. We could handle this. We were not surprised to be given glasses of water with ice in them, almost as soon as we sat down. We were delighted; this was what we had been told would happen in New York, and it had happened.

The hamburger came, and with it a plastic squeeze bottle full of tomato ketchup. Less delightful, but also to be expected. I decided I would prefer mustard, and asked for some. About a minute later, 1 the air moved slightly near my cheek, and there was a light thump as a packet of mustard hit the tabletop. After a moment's panic I turned, but the waiter was already gone, out of our ambit. The mustard lay, yellow in its transparent covering, on the table between us. It was an individual serving, just for me and not for Colin, who had not asked for any. The packet was soft and cool; the mustard was ready mixed. You were expected to tear the packet open and squeeze the mustard out with your fingers – but I could not bring myself to do that yet. We sat and looked at the mustard missile, and knew that we had reached a foreign place, an unpredictable and infinitely weird environment, which we had not come from, and into which we would slot ourselves only eventually and with the utmost difficulty. That packet of mustard was my introduction to North America.

I have been trying to understand what we participate in and what is going on around us ever since. I find, after thirty years of this, that I have fiercely guarded my original puzzled, anxious state, for it sharpens my vision and never lets my curiosity relax. I have also kept trying to understand things (like mustard packets) and behaviour (like flinging the mustard down and hurrying on), because I have found that specificities reveal principles: by focusing on small, humble, taken-for-granted objects and demeanours you can tease out of them philosophies, choices, prejudices, causes, contradictions, tragedies, absurdities. I refuse to accept the ordinary as dull: common things – it stands to reason – are the most important things, the ones with history and politics and meaning, the ones with clout.

In our 'consumer' culture, we are constantly confronted with crowds of objects and with changing fashions in behaviour. The simultaneity and repetitiousness of the bombardment, the multiplicity of the things and the speed with which they reach their targets, serve to make them inscrutable to us, and exhausting in their apparent self-sufficiency and dynamism. Finally they can come to seem meaningless, and boring. But they are *there*, and they keep on requiring us to negotiate with them, even if only to find a way to keep out of their reach. My project is to grab some of them as they hurtle by. I seize one of them at a time, hold it still, and look at it closely to see where it comes from and what it might be hiding. It is important to know how we are all implicated in the existence of these culturally resonant objects, and in their form.

Talking Turkey

'Rugose and carunculated,' Audubon called its head and neck: all wrinkly and covered with flabby wattles, warts, tubercles, and bumps. The weirdest of a turkey's fifty or so caruncles is attached to its face; in the male this cone of flesh, drooping over its bill, can stretch in a trice from one to ten centimetres in length.

The whole featherless neck and head changes colour as the turkey's moods alter, from white to turquoise to blue, to pink, purple, orange, and flaming red. When the male is courting, the flat skin of his neck is red and the warty caruncles brilliant blue. The bird gobbles; he struts and puffs (the latter performance is called a *pfum*), and his tail feathers display in the manner of a peacock.

The Indians used the feathers for headdresses, arrows, and fans, or twisted them on cords and wove them into cloaks and highly efficient blankets. The male has a black bristle 'beard' hanging from his chest, which was used to sprinkle water in religious ceremonies.

Columbus encountered the bird first on an island off the coast of Honduras, where the Indians served some to him roasted; at other Indian feasts the Spaniards were offered vast tamales containing a whole turkey each. The appearance of the living birds astounded, fascinated, and confused the Europeans, who ended up calling the creature *Meleagris gallopavo*: 'guineafowl chickenpeacock'.

The popular name varies from Indian tribe to tribe, and from country to country. The English thought the huge new chicken originated in Turkey, and the French and Italians named it 'from India' (*dinde* and *gallo d'India*); the Turks themselves called it *hindi*. Persians said it was a *filmurgh* or 'elephant bird', because of its size and maybe also because of the main caruncle; and the Japanese, awed perhaps by all those changing wattles, call it *shichimencho*: 'seven-faced'.

Turkeys are extraordinarily primitive fowl in certain respects. They seem never to think of looking down when seeking an escape route, and their eyeballs fit so tightly into their sockets that they have to turn their heads to see moving objects. A deafened 5 female turkey, hearing no sound from her young, will take them for foreign pests and peck them to death; and a turkey with mud on its head may be murdered by its brethren for looking odd. The birds can become enraged by unusual rocks or old bones; at any unexpected noise all males and some females gobble madly. Their stupidity has become proverbial: in eighteenth-century France *dindonné* meant 'duped', like English 'gulled'; and calling somebody 'a turkey' today is ruder still.

The position of the female's head and neck is essential in turkey mating: cocks will display before a disembodied hen's head crudely carved in wood, provided the thing is held at precisely the seductive angle. Turkeys can reproduce by parthenogenesis (eggs may hatch young without sex), which places them early on the avian evolutionary chain.

The wild turkey is almost extinct in its pure state; it is believed that nearly all those now being carefully conserved in the wild have some admixture of domestic blood. Wild turkeys roamed eastern North America in flocks of thousands when the Europeans arrived. They squatted in the trees, huge and utterly unafraid of human beings; in many Indian tribes adult men scorned to hunt them, leaving turkey-catching to children because they were such easy game.

Turkeys were shot with so much abandon by the European settlers that their numbers declined rapidly. As early as 1672, John Josselyn wondered whether wild turkeys might soon disappear forever. There was a tremendous loss of habitat, including a large-scale depletion of ginseng berries, one of the favourite foods of turkeys. Ginseng plants and roots were exported for excellent prices to the Chinese market.

Mexican Indians had domesticated the turkey in pre-Columbian times. The U.S. and Canada, however, got domestic turkeys not from Central America but from England and France, where they were bred from birds imported from Spain. Almost as soon as they reached Europe, turkeys began to supplant peacocks, and eventually geese, as the 'great birds' traditionally eaten at Christmas and other celebrations. Turkeys are impressively large and turn golden with basting; their capacious insides inspire creativity in the stuffing.

Turkey breasts were an instant favourite with American and Canadian colonists, who often dried, ground, and kneaded the powdered meat to make 7 cheap and easy 'bread'. Geneticists have grossly enlarged the turkey's breast. They have also made the bird delicate, susceptible to cold and wet, almost incapable of copulating (fertilization has to be achieved with human help), and sometimes unsteady on its feet because of its bulging *embonpoint*.

The meat it offers is not only light, the most preferred, but also dark, which lends variety. Darkness in bird meat comes from the myoglobin which stores oxygen for muscles; the breasts of game birds are dark because they fly. Legs are dark in the domesticated turkey because even battery-raised birds have to stand, and so make use of the muscles in their legs.

In eighteenth-century Europe and North America, long before refrigeration and swift transport, flocks of turkeys were commonly walked a hundred miles or more to market so that they could be slaughtered when and where they were bought and eaten. From the large breeding farms in Norfolk thousands of birds crowded down the narrow roads to London during the weeks preceding Christmas.

The great black Norfolk gobblers (which the English called 'bubbly-jocks') wore shoes for the journey. Their feet were dipped in thick pitch, tied up in sacking, or covered with little boots to protect them on the long noisy march south. Dark meat must definitely have predominated by the time turkeys arrived upon city dinner tables.

Avocados

High in the cloud forests of northern South America, the fruit grows to the size of a large olive; it is beloved of two-toed sloths and named by botanists *nubigena*, 'the cloud-born'. In the region of Mount Popocatepetl, Mexican Indians worked long and hard upon another race of the same tree and perfected a somewhat larger, thin-skinned, purple version, with a scent like anise. These two, hybridized in pre-Columbian times, eventually created the big green avocado usually for sale in northern cities today.

The purple parent is the most ancient cultivated one; it was being grown by the peoples of Central America before 7000 BC. Gradually the fruit improved through selection, but avocado trees grow so slowly and their seeds produce so erratically that a sudden great leap forward in the fruit's size, which occurred around 900 BC, is considered to be proof of a significant increase in social organization among the people who produced them.

The results are still popular in Mexico today, and their taste is greatly preferred among gourmets who have tried all the varieties. But 'Mexican' avocados are not exported north, both because they are small and because their thin skins make them difficult to transport without bruising. The ones we get are crossed with the 'Guatemalan' type, direct descendants of the wild and thick-skinned *nubigena*.

There is one more domesticated type of avocado – the so-called 'West Indian', which also originated in Mexico. It is a tropical version (the other two are subtropical), and the trees now flourish in the Caribbean, in Florida, in Africa, and in other hot parts of the world. The one growing in our garden in Zambia was nearly forty feet tall. This fruit's skin is purple, and you can tell the fruit is ripe because its pip loosens: you shake it, and take it if you hear the pip bumping around inside.

Tropical avocados are only three to ten per cent fat, as opposed to anything up to thirty per cent in the types preferring cooler conditions. There is more oil in avocados than in any other fruit except olives. The oil is highly digestible, and chemically very like olive oil; its main use so far is in cosmetic creams. Avocados, like grapefruit, have become for us a popular pre-dinner appetizer; but in Brazil they are preferred sugared and eaten for dessert.

The fruit is an anomaly in many ways. Maturation, for instance, does not change its skin colour, and the fruit does not soften until it has left the tree. Readiness for harvesting is therefore determined by trial and error, or by chemical tests for oil content. A mature avocado can be 'stored' for weeks, and sometimes up to seven months, simply by being left on the tree. Picking the fruit cuts off the hormone (produced in the leaves) that prevents it from ripening.

Three or four days afterwards the avocado will be ready to eat, a state recognizable when it is slightly soft at the stem end; but this happens only if it has (imperceptibly) matured on the tree. Mild refrigeration keeps the fruit another month or so after harvesting. But the avocado, unlike any other fruit, needs oxygen in order to ripen without spoiling; it must not be wrapped up while it is metabolizing. Another rule is that fruit usually sweetens as it matures; but the ripening process in the avocado actually *reduces* sugar content, to as little as one per cent.

Animals, even carnivores, love avocados. Père Labat describes in his Caribbean journal (1693–

1705) how wild pigs from miles around would congregate under the avocado trees when a windstorm had shaken the fruit to the ground. 'These animals,' he wrote, 'become in consequence marvellously plump, and their flesh contracts an excellent savour.'

Dipping chips and bits of vegetable into a centrally placed bowl of sauce is a distinctively North American table trait. The practice expresses informality, individuality, and egalitarianism, of course – but it may also derive historically from the American Indian habit of adding enriching sauces to the corn staple of the region: corn needs supplements in order to be adequately nutritious. One of the best sauce-making fruits on earth was ready to hand in Central America: the buttery, mashable, protein- and vitamin-rich avocado. Modern North Americans discovered it relatively recently; when they did, their dipping habit was already ingrained.

Europe received its first large supplies from Israel in the 1970s. Israelis have heartily adopted and promoted them, developing special harvesting machinery, experimenting with recipes, and introducing the idea of weaning babies on avocado flesh.

The name of the fruit in Spanish is *aguacate*,

earlier *ahuacate*, fruit of *ahuacacuahatl*, the Aztec 'testicle tree': pear-shaped fruit hang from the tree in pairs. *Avocado* may also have been influenced by the Spanish word for a delicacy, *bocado*. When Jamaicans received the avocado, nearly 300 years before North Americans began seriously growing it, they turned *ahuacate* into *alligator* because the word had an easier and more familiar sound.

North Americans popularly called them *alligator pears* until marketers decided the connotations were a turn-off, and pushed the term *avocado*. Indian claims for aphrodisiac powers in the fruit were hotly denied when it was first being introduced widely in North America at the beginning of this century; the reputation is no longer thought by the industry to be a liability.

Caviar

One way of getting rid of the huge fish was to pile them up like cordwood on the beach and let the oil seep out of their bodies; you then set the whole heap alight. Each adult sturgeon was between three and six feet long, and could weigh over 200 pounds. In Canada in the 1850s they were worth about ten cents apiece – if you could find a buyer. It was hardly worth cutting them up, even for pig-feed. For one thing, sturgeon carry bony plates on the *outside* of their bodies. These, sharp and spiny in the young, tore up the fishing nets that were trying to bring up valuable whitefish and lake trout; the enormous adults, whose plates had worn smooth, just weighed everything down.

A great deal of hard work went into clearing North American lakes of sturgeon. People would spear them as they passed slowly under a bridge on their way to spawn; they would drag a harpooned fish up by the rope, which would cause it nearly always to split or burst. The method was fairly effective, but unpleasant because of the eggs. The gravid females were absolutely crammed with eggs – about twenty-five pounds per fish. These would splatter all over the bridge, and soon begin to stink like hell.

Eggs rather like those are still to be found. Today, however, they travel, carefully refrigerated, all the way from Russia or Iran. During the 1980s, a small glass pot of them could cost about forty-five dollars – that's about fifteen dollars per teaspoon. And caviar, the roe of the sturgeon (no other fish gives real caviar), is still one of the most expensive food-stuffs in the world.

It is served up on sculpted ice, or in *présentoirs* of glass and silver with crushed-ice compartments. It should be eaten in solitary grandeur (never *ever* add *anything* to caviar, not even a drop of lemon juice) with a special long-handled spoon made of horn, mother-of-pearl, ivory, or gold. (Any metal other than gold ruins caviar.) A tiny piece of toast, upon which you lift the precious burden with your fingers, is permissible.

Always, caviar is accompanied by the metal lid which is its hallmark of authenticity. It is beluga, sevruga, or osetra, it comes from the Caspian Sea, and it is *malossol*, treated to 'little salt'. The only correct accompaniments are iced vodka (some recommend a bottle covered in moulded ice – a little slippery, one would have thought) or champagne: 'To celebrate the sublime, summon only the perfect.'

Caviar has always been greatly admired in Russia – as has the flesh of the sturgeon. The first fish and eggs of the season belonged to the Tsar. *Acipenser* (now its zoological name) was a noble fish in ancient Rome: it was served up adorned with wreaths by slaves themselves crowned with greenery, and to the accompaniment of flutes. An unrepealed British law keeps sturgeon and whales, like swans, the perquisites of the monarch. The salted eggs, even when sturgeon abounded, were always the acquired taste of an élite: what most people could not appreciate was 'caviar to the general'. (In Shakespeare's day the word was both spelled and pronounced 'cauiarie,' with the accent on the first syllable.)

The real mystique of caviar (as opposed to sturgeon meat) began in the West only in 1920. It was invented by two Russo-Armenian brothers, Melkom and Mougcheg Petrossian, who had escaped to Paris during the Revolution. Realizing that caviar was not to be had in their new country, they simply telephoned Moscow and demanded some. They also asked for commercial rights to sixty-three per cent of Russian caviar exports – a privilege the family still enjoys.

At the Gastronomic Exhibition at the Grand Palais in 1920, Melkom and Mougcheg gave free tastings – and provided large pans for spitting out what most of the uninitiated could not stomach. It was a huge success: crowds came to watch the grimaces, cheer on the brave, and marvel at the rapturous few and at the price they were prepared to pay for salted fish eggs. The slot that many societies keep for one outrageously overvalued foodstuff was filled. Caviar is expensive, fabled, exotic, difficult to prepare, to keep, to transport, and to eat. It is also increasingly rare. The combination is irresistible.

The race of sturgeon, one of the great armoured fishes of the upper Cretaceous, survived in enormous numbers for over a hundred million years – until the mid-nineteenth century. The sturgeon is a scavenger on lake bottoms; it has no natural enemies. But the fact is that the wanton destruction of sturgeon by our ancestors looks benign when set beside the damage being done to them at present. In North America the few remaining sturgeon are threatened by the contaminated sediment that drains into lakes and rivers and settles there, increasingly blanketing their feeding grounds and killing off the crabs and clams they eat. The Caspian Sea itself is sinking because of dams, and pollution is tainting its waters.

We all see the need to save the sturgeon: North America has actually set up committees to discuss the remaining stocks. It would be a pity to waste those gold and ivory teaspoons. We could always, of course, reduce something else to rarity instead.

Wedding Cake

Weddings revolve around brides. Wearing her extraordinary clothes, flanked by 'maids' in costume, waited upon, stared at, toasted, envied, and admired, a woman who becomes 'the bride' for a day must necessarily steal the show. Even the groom is merely a bridegroom ('the bride's man'), and in the past in Britain there were also the bride bed, the bride ale, many small cakes, and finally a single large one called 'the bride cake'. Its name changed to 'wedding cake' during the nineteenth century.

A bride cake was round, flat like an oatcake, and spiced. An early custom was, after the ritual of the ring, to break the cake over the bride's head. This invoked fertility, as where brides in several different cultures are showered with rice, 'many small things', signifying a fecund future. Breaking the cake was also figurative of the end of the bride's maidenhead.

Modern wedding cakes in the Anglo-Saxon tradition are not designed to maintain this ritual. They are huge and gorgeous creations, one of the major expenses of a 'white' wedding. A wedding cake may be piped with scrolls, scattered with icing flowers, studded with pearls and silver balls, beribboned, caged in a shiny sugar filigree, and topped with a nosegay of fresh flowers or porcelain figurines of the bride and her groom.

Wedding cakes mount in tiers, cake upon cake; they can reach a height of eight feet, and even sport a fountain at the top, made to descend, without wetting the cake, via aqueducts to a pumping device that forces the water up to fall again. The top tier of the cake (the littlest one) may be kept for the christening party of the couple's first child, or to celebrate the first anniversary of the wedding: fruitcakes can be expected, with care, to last a year. Americans prefer sponges, even cheesecakes, which are light and resolutely ephemeral.

The English cake derives from three main traditions: the ancient plum pudding or dried fruit concoction symbolic of festive plenty; the small almond-paste, iced 'marchpanes' of the Renaissance, which gave us the distinctive double icing; and the medieval 'subtlety'. 'Subtleties' were bravura pieces, created to surprise and delight noble guests. They were served at banquets as a form of entertainment, and included such fantasies as sugar sculptures, and four-and-twenty blackbirds baked in a pie. (Stag parties are said still to boast of ladies leaping out of cardboard cakes.)

Our wedding cakes are almost the last of the great culinary pyramids and constructions that used to be in such demand at feasts. Since the early twentieth century in Britain, the tiers have been lifted on pillars. (Upturned champagne-glasses are now a popular variant.) Americans prefer sugar fondant to almond paste, and cakes that maintain the older ziggurat form because soft cake cannot support pillars. Upper layers of soft cake are held up by a system of wooden dowels and cardboard plateaux disguised with piped icing or ribbon. Canadians participate in both traditions. The fruitcake group often insist on making their own layers from a family recipe, bringing the results to be mounted on pillars and iced by professionals.

The bride can share her luck by tossing her bouquet or giving guests bits of her cake. Girls used to take these home and sleep with them under their pillows to induce dreams of future husbands. The sharing of the cake now tends to be honed severely, to save time. The bottom layer is often all the cake there is, serving only as matter for the first ritual cut, and, in America, the sharing of the first slice between bride and groom; the other layers are made of iced styrofoam. Sometimes the whole edifice is fake; ready-sliced and even boxed bits of real cake are brought separately and handed out to guests. We should 'not even discuss' putting wedding cake under our pillows, according to one master confectioner – hers admittedly being of the *génoise* and cheesecake variety.

But there is no wedding without photographs of the bride and groom together Cutting the Cake. The custom spread in the 1930s, when dense British cakes were encased in extra-hard white icing, to hold up the pillared layers. Grooms 'helped' brides to cut the cake with a beribboned knife or sword. Now the pair perform as a team. The cake stands tall, white, archaic, and decorated, pyramidal like the veiled bride herself, and dominating the proceedings; it is a version of the bride, and the piercing of it dramatizes her rite of passage.

Menus

For human beings, a meal is never just something to eat: language tends always to get into the act. A written restaurant menu is a semiotic construct, a food-related literary composition that exists not merely to inform clients of what they may ask for and how much it will cost. It enculturates a meal by drawing attention to the inherent ranking and order of the proceedings, and it also impresses, stimulates, and even intimidates its readers. A menu insinuates far more than it actually says.

In the western world, menus have commonly been provided to the diners at feasts since the early nineteenth century. The custom previously was to lay all the dishes out in front of the guests, tell them what everything was, its age, provenance, and manner of preparation, and then to let people pick what they wanted. Our buffets partly preserve the tradition. Menus, on the other hand, are like theatre programmes, listing courses that will appear from behind the scenes, in plotted sequence. Everybody gets the same food; choice is a matter merely of quantity or of abstention from what is proffered on the platter at one's elbow.

Restaurant menus do offer choices, at prices. Modern commercial menu practice is heavily researched and wickedly sophisticated. It begins with texture: our senses are aroused and readied, apparently, by padded leather covers, glossy embossments, trailing tassels. (Black is 'tasteful', orange 'opulent', while mere string says 'farm'.) A precautionary plastic sleeve covering the text gives a robust message, as does deckle-edged rag paper: it all depends on the restaurant's image, which we unconsciously ingest with our fingertips as we ruminate on what to have.

The menu might reflect the restaurant's décor, and be trimmed with a motif repeated on napkins, tablecloths, curtains; it might even reproduce a photograph of an unpolluted landscape, or pictures suggesting the 'life-styles' of the rich and thin. A tall narrow menu, often white and with clean-cut modern artwork, says 'cities; slick, up-to-the-minute, and speedy'; a broad format in unbleached – even speckled or recycled – paper with rustic writing means country cooking, regional tradition, maternal meals near warm ancestral stoves.

Some menus are hand-written, perhaps in French Bistro 'licked pencil' purple, or chalked on blackboards. These suggest a repertoire spontaneously inspired by the catch of the day, out of simple yet rich stores of honest tradition. Conflicting messages – stability plus change, fun with a solid background – are offered by a heavy durable folder with an apparently ever-new paper list (it must be very clean) slipped inside.

Some food-industry advisers recommend that patrons be allowed to take cheaply produced menus away with them: they are travelling advertisements, almost as obliging as lettered T-shirts (provide those too, if you can). Remember that the lower left quadrant of an opened menu is what seizes the eye first and most securely: put your most popular 'anchor items' there, and price them low, because first-time customers most often choose those, and might come back. (Do not put stuffed peppers or strange shellfish concoctions there, for it is a rare clientele that dotes on risk.) More desserts are sold by waiters than by menus: leave the desserts off the menu, and make your staff try them all, then recite their names and properties to guests. Pay waiters a percentage of every dessert sold.

Describe, describe, describe; even print short recipes, especially for complex drinks. Everything must be done to *name*, and then to complete the key ingredients with connotations: many a sale has been clinched by a phrase like 'slowly baked to a golden brown' or 'bite-sized, plump, sautéed in butter, and served atop steaming linguine'. Give imaginative titles to your dishes, if possible incorporating the restaurant's name, to add distinction and aid the memory. 'Elite operations' are assured that they may still use French; it sometimes causes questions to be asked, and provides an opportunity for the waiters to deploy their training and talents.

Menus, dealing as they do with food, pluck highly sensitive chords in all of us. For this very reason, menu 'typos' and howlers are some of the funniest in the genre, especially when, as a nervous foreigner, one encounters the efforts of restaurants abroad to say everything in English. My collection includes a Venetian *bollito misto* translated as 'mixed boils', and a Turkish list that offered, among other treats, 'roast dust' and 'tart of the house'.

Vinegar and the Search for Sour

We taste sour things mostly along the sides of our tongues, which are able to detect one sour part in 130,000. Why we are so quick to notice sourness is unknown. The ability to taste salt and sweetness evolved to induce us to eat substances that nutrition requires; our extreme sensitivity to bitterness (we notice one part in 2,000,000) alerts us to most poisons. Taste, however, does not always detect acids reliably: the acid in citrus fruit, for instance, metabolizes at once, while corn and lentils are actually acid-forming. But sourness does cause us to salivate, and there is no tasting without saliva.

As we grow up we learn to turn somewhat from sweet, and to savour the sharpness in many foods. (Sourness, in all languages, is described as 'pointy'.) Human societies have throughout history sought out and cultivated sour stuffs. The British, for instance, prized gooseberries, sorrel (the first syllable of which means 'sour'), and verjuice (it 28 rhymed with 'charges'), the juice of sour grapes reduced to the consistency of honey. Lemon juice replaced verjuice in Europe during the eighteenth century.

Wine left open to warm air was either ruined, or mysteriously changed into a delicious acid condiment that added excitement to sauces, meat, and bland leaves, and could preserve foods by pickling. Cider and malt vinegars complemented the soured milks and sauerkraut of northern climates; but vinegar, most strictly and most nobly, is soured wine, as the name shows: it is from the French, *vin aigre*.

In 1777 the French chemist Lavoisier gave oxygen a name that means in Greek 'acid begetter', because he thought that souring was the gas's main function. Oxygen in the air is indeed required in making vinegar as opposed to spoiled wine, but for a reason Lavoisier could not have imagined. After a preliminary fermentation, vinegar is created by a host of single-celled mushrooms, each one one-thousandth of a millimetre in diameter, that gather on the surface of the wine, feed on oxygen and on alcohol, and turn the latter into acid. They form a thin raft of bacteria, a floating 'fungus skin', or mycoderm.

Sometimes accidents happen – the surface of the 29

souring wine is jolted, or tiny vinegar eels are born in the liquid, rise to the surface for air, and cling, round the edges of the barrel, to the mycoderm veil. The troubled film falls into the vinegar and forms a weird slithery blob, a zoogloea, which will die for want of oxygen.

In the past, vinegar-making methods involved deep reverence for this rubbery mass. It was called a 'mother of vinegar' and was transferred carefully to new batches of souring wine to work its magic. Each 'mother' had its own greatly valued gustatory properties. It was handed down as a family heirloom, or fiercely guarded by professional *vinaigriers*.

We now know that the real 'mother' was not the submerged blob but the film on top of the liquid. The sacred 'mothers', lifted out of the vinegar, carried a little made vinegar and bits of the living veil with them, to ferment, grow again, and impart their particular flavours to the next batches of wine. The barrels, soaked in vinegar and bacteria, helped a good deal, as did the quality of the local wine. *Acetobacter*, the vinegar bacterium, travels relentlessly, which is why spilt wine must be mopped up at once in a winery. Vinegar casks are often kept in an entirely separate building from precious aging wines.

Most vinegar is now sold as the background to a myriad of bottled salad dressings, mayonnaises, pickles, and sauces. Tomato ketchup accounts for ten per cent of all vinegar made in North America. The process of pickling preserves vegetables, but we eat most of them in summer, when other vegetables are plentiful: we love pickles for their taste, in itself. Vinegar is a mild disinfectant, and used to be extremely useful for wiping over the body to discourage fleas.

Nowadays wine vinegar, and herbed or balsamic vinegar, have become expensive gourmet treats. Most vinegar on supermarket shelves has nothing to do with extraordinary aromas or with wine; it is made very quickly, by pumping and percolating raw white spirit through wood shavings soaked in acetic acid, and diluting the result in water.

Christmas Pudding

Festival foods with staying power must make us feel that they are old and strange, yet typically ours. They should involve some time and if possible several people in their preparation, and if we can be persuaded to eat them only on the festival day itself, so much the better. For Anglo-Saxons, Christmas pudding fulfils all the conditions.

The pudding is only about two centuries old, but it feels much older. And indeed it is possible to find ancient roots for it – in meat soups and humble medieval wheat gruels. Another component in the story was a great sausage, called 'hackin' because of the minced or 'hacked' meat enclosed in its skin. French *boudin*, 'sausage', is related to the English word 'pudding'. And real Christmas pudding still must contain the meat-fat, suet.

Only very recently has the Western European culinary tradition habitually separated meat from sweetness. Sugar used to be classed as a spice along with salt; and fruit often accompanied meat. In the seventeenth century, Britain began importing a lot more dried fruit than formerly: prunes from France, currants from Greece (the word derives from 'Corinth'), sultanas from Turkey. These were added to meat and grain soups for feasts; the result was a thick 'plum porridge'. Gradually it became uncommon to include prunes; the word 'plum' stuck, however, as a general term for dried fruit.

A momentous invention for British cuisine was the pudding-cloth (late seventeenth century). It did away with guts and paunches as bags to hold food, as they still do only for sausages and haggis. Most family meals were cooked over the hearth fire, in a hanging cauldron. The meat was boiled in liquid, and to it were added vegetables, and balls of pudding wrapped in buttered cloth. Savoury puddings were often eaten as a separate course, after the soup and before the meat. 'No broth no ball, no ball no beef,' children were admonished: one had to eat soup, then carbohydrate staple, then meat, in that order. Meat was expensive – not to be gobbled down with an unblunted appetite.

'Plum porridge', stiffened, could also be boiled in a pudding cloth and eaten for dessert. Made richer, denser, and heavy with fruit, it became festive, and in the end exclusively Christmas, fare. Rich people, who could afford the luxury of oven baking, also made cakes at Christmas: the Twelfth Cakes of Epiphany, January 6.

At this feast of the Magi, trinkets such as rings, money, and charms, symbolic of future events, were secreted in the cake, to be found by chance (or fate) in the portions served. A bean in one's cake made one king for the day; the custom was part of the saturnalian aspect of Christmas, where children rule and royalty can be conferred on anyone at random. In the late nineteenth century, Twelfth Cakes began to die out, leaving echoes in the iced Christmas cake – and in the coins buried in Christmas pudding.

The pudding was simpler and cheaper than the cake, and everyone had the equipment needed to cook it. Its shape was spherical until recently, and it was considered patriotically British. No foreigners could make it successfully (many stories tell how they try, but forget for example to wrap it in the pudding-cloth first); nor could they stomach its stodge. There is swaggering, even military symbolism too: Pepys ate 'a mess of brave plum-porridge' to open his Christmas dinner in 1662; and Dickens

in *A Christmas Carol* describes one 'like a speckled

cannon-ball, so hard and firm, blazing in half of half-a-quartern of ignited brandy . . .'

The burning alcohol gives the dark, rich pudding a singular, extravagant yet elemental air; the fire lasts only a short time, as befits festival magic. Traditionally, the pudding took plenty of time to make, however. The ones home-made from old family recipes were prepared between July and October so they could be properly aged for Christmas; they were stirred by every member of the family, from east to west in honour of the journey of the Magi. Our own Christmas puddings are likely to be shop-bought sometime in December, and enclosed in covered basins rather than in pudding-cloths. They can be steamed or boiled still; or callously zapped in a microwave by those of us for whom the annual roast-with-trimmings is quite enough to cope with.

Unreasonably solid, fatty, sweet, rotund, calorie-laden, and lathered with brandy butter, the pudding is served once – and only once – a year. It amounts to an outrageous snub to everything thin, new, light, and mobile. An obstinate cannon-ball from the past, the Christmas pudding intractably sits there, mocking the very idea of modernity.

Broad Beans

Nearly all the beans we eat, except for Asian or African varieties, come originally from America – whether they be haricot, lima, kidney, navy, green or 'French', 'Roman', or 'Tuscan'. The Old World's bean was the fava or broad bean, which was cultivated before 6000 BC. Until the sixteenth century AD any European reference to beans – for counting, to mean something of little value as in 'a hill of beans', as gaming pieces, to cure warts, as well as for eating – invariably means broad beans.

Ripe broad beans are brown (Homer's 'dark-skinned' beans), and fed to horses. Bean-fed horses grow sleek and frisky; stable slang is the source of our expression 'full of beans'. People eat fava bean-seeds green, unpeeled, and even raw if young enough, or with their greyish skins removed when a little older. They taste rather like green peas. Fava bean-seeds are also dried, and later soaked and cooked. The month of May in modern Rome is welcomed with ecstatically downed dishes of fresh baby favas and glasses of cold Frascati.

Mediterranean peoples eat broad beans constantly – favas may well be their oldest cultivated vegetable – yet they have looked askance at them for millennia. For one thing, they cause flatulence; for another they grow eerily fast; and when you peel one the bare green bean looks like a human embryo, with tiny but distinct male sexual organs.

The great sage and mathematician Pythagoras demanded strict vegetarianism from his ascetic followers; and in addition they were to follow his famous command, '*Abstain from beans!*' Since they were like little human beings, rejecting beans as food underwrote the vast taboo against cannibalism. Eating them was like eating 'the heads of your parents'. (The idea that beans are 'heads' survives in modern English slang: to 'bean' someone is to hit them on the head; one used to hear people addressing each other as 'old bean'; the word 'beanie' means a little hat.)

The ancients believed that soul (*psyche, anima*) was breath, life breathed into us at creation. Flatulence, therefore, was angry dead souls (ingested in fava beans) fighting for an exit. People might also have imagined some of their own souls as well being farted inadvertently away. Words for beans (*kuamoi* in Greek, *iwryt* in Egyptian) echoed verbs meaning 'conceive': flatulence was a swift and sinister pregnancy.

Beans were also known to cause strange malevolent dreams. Ancient Greeks, and especially the Pythagoreans, were deeply interested in dream analysis, and among the consequences of eating fava beans was a warping of the truth that dreams were trying to announce to the dreamer, or even dreams that were downright false. Eating beans resulted in perturbation and pollution – what sages and sensible people strive to avoid.

Democracy, in Athens, involved choosing magistrates *by lot*: chance was enlisted as a means of eliminating graft. Drawn lots were fateful decisions, with a 'will' of their own. Perhaps for this reason, beans were used to draw lots; when voting 'yes' or 'no', in contrast, Athenians used black or white pebbles. Some sources suggest that 'abstaining from beans' might also have meant not offering oneself for public office. (Beans as 'lots' survive in the Twelfth Night Cake or *gâteau des rois*, where he who finds a bean in his slice is king for the day.)

All through history, especially in Mediterranean lands where broad beans inspire both love and ambivalence, some people have found that they suffer after eating broad beans: headaches, laboured breathing, fever, back or stomach pain, even, in children, death. The condition was named for the first time in 1894: *favism*, after the beans.

The main facts about favism were not understood till 1957. Some people, almost all of them males, inherit (through their mothers) a metabolic defect in a red blood cell enzyme, known as glucose-6-phosphate dehydrogenase deficiency. They react badly to eating broad beans – even to breathing in their pollen. (Pythagoras, it is remembered, warned his followers not even to walk through a beanfield.) The official discovery of favism adds an explanation that can satisfy the modern mind as to why this particular vegetable in folk wisdom has always been represented as either haunted or ritually taboo.

It is strange that the very people who suffer most from favism (which is almost unknown in many other places) are also the ones who eat the most broad beans. But researchers point out that the beans contain several substances used today in drugs to combat malaria. This protection, the theory goes, for the Mediterranean peoples who were often in danger of contracting malaria, was important enough in the normal population for fava beans to remain a staple crop in spite of their danger for some.

Chicken: From Jungle Fowl to Patties

Carving up a whole animal, whether a chicken or an ox, has from time immemorial expressed not only family feeling and cohesion among the people sharing that animal, but also hierarchy and difference. In ancient Greece, for example, an animal eaten in common was a symbol of the organization of the group, and indeed of society itself, in its diversity as well as its wholeness. A pig or an ox has only four legs, one liver, two haunches, and so on: it is impossible for everyone to receive the same cut of meat. Many traditions have assigned status to various cuts; it mattered deeply which piece you got, and it usually fell to the head man to be the carver, who 'did the honours' and assigned to each person his 'portion', which could be broadly representative of his kinship or friendship status, and of his lot in life. Our society will have none of that – and nothing more directly expresses ourloathing of hierarchy than the pre-cut, pre-coated, ground-and-reconstituted portions, often computer-calculated to be equal, which we get as fast food.

At our meal, which is an old-fashioned home-cooked affair with a whole roast chicken as the meat portion of its main course, each guest will state his preference, for drumstick or breast, white or dark meat. We shall murmur our choices, yet almost always assent to what we are offered. Older women and men will be consulted first; but a good carver (the role still tends to be played by a male) will endeavour to save at least a little breast for everyone.

European settlers brought to North America the tradition that eating fowl was special – behaviour both ceremonial and festive. Rich families ate roast chicken, shared out by the knife-wielding chief male of the family, on Sundays. King Henri IV of France had in the sixteenth century pronounced the ideal of extending this universally desired luxury to everybody: 'I hope to make France so prosperous that every peasant will have a chicken in his pot on Sundays.' Americans worked hard to turn the occasional treat into an everyday occurrence, as well as to make it available to all. In 1928 the Republican Party won an election in the United States with the help of the slogan, 'A chicken in every pot': even the limitation to periodicity had been broken. As chicken became increasingly common, the role of the roasted festive fowl fell more often to the turkey, which was winged, feathered, and fattened, and could be roasted to an elaborate gold like a chicken, but which was much more impressive in size, with a larger capacity for special stuffings. A whole roast chicken can still exude some of its former stylish glory, however. Indeed, the facts that it is pale meat and perceived as 'light' have recently added to its prestige.

The knife-and-fork revolution which swept Europe in the sixteenth and seventeenth centuries never entirely conquered the eating of fowl. Bird meat is much easier to disengage from the bone with the teeth than with a knife and fork; drumsticks and wings seem almost made to be held. So the paradox arose that chicken, which for a long time was made the centrepiece of meals on special occasions, was quite often the only meat people were commonly allowed to treat with the utter informality of handling it at table.

In North America, especially in the southern United States, there arose a strong preference for fried chicken: fowl cut up in advance instead of being ceremonially carved before the assembled group. Chicken in pieces became one of the original American 'finger foods', eaten on occasions where formality is sacrificed to relaxed conviviality, together with sandwiched food, corn on the cob, and food hand-dipped in sauces. Modern fast foods greatly encourage the banishment of knives and forks; informality as well as speed require it. (An important secondary consideration, one which is more frequently expressed by fast-food managers, is that removing cutlery means there is nothing to steal.)

Fried and crumbed chicken pieces have been marketed as fast foods with huge success, for poultry, especially modern fast-grown chicken meat, is bland and acceptable to almost every palate. It can even claim to be unfattening and a 'low-cholesterol' food, because fowl fat (except in capons) does not marble the meat, but lines the body immediately under the skin and is contained in pockets, so that it is easily removed. Yet, in spite of chicken's many strong points in modern schemes of taste, the poultry industry has produced such enormous amounts of meat that new ways of eating chicken

have been urgently sought in order to whet demand.

The fact is that the chicken, in order to become absolutely malleable and modern, has had to escape its intractable shape. What used to be the source of its symbolism – the differentiation embodied by a whole trussed fowl – has become an anachronistic defect. Even pre-cut, fried chicken pieces constitute a somewhat limited answer: choices still have to be made and distinctions drawn. A deboning process has now been perfected, and this has opened up a vast new future for the chicken. Boneless meat is available for chicken sticks, chicken rolls, chicken frankfurters, and chicken chunks. The beef hamburger, which is still the centre and focus of the fast-food industry, is being challenged by a new technological feat: the cheap, light, springy (the word is that of poultry scientists) chicken pattie with its machine-tooled shape, square, circular, or oblong. Scientific articles commonly call it 'restructured steak'.

Fast-food outlets are cultural institutions dedicated not only to dealing swiftly with mankind's compulsion to eat and drink regularly, but also to doing battle with his twin and fatal limitations of space and time. The campaign is waged with the weapons of the industrial and technological age; its driving force is our own particular and paradoxical blend of obsessive rationality and relaxed asceticism.

Fast foods are processed and sold by giant industrial complexes which control every detail of their operations, from the smallest ingredient to the carefully calculated appearance of every eating place. The goal is to give an impression of the omnipresence and the invariability of McDonald's or of Kentucky Fried: travel as far as you like, and it will always be as though you were still at home, in the arms of the parent company. Space loses its ancient association with change and surprise. You can without difficulty seek out the identical ambience, the very same taste you knew and liked before you set out.

These parent companies are called 'chains'. When you travel (and mobility is another of our cultural institutions), they provide links which render your route as predictable and as secure, as protective and as limiting as swaddling bands. It is no accident that both the kind of food they sell and their marketing methods make a direct appeal to the infantile in all of us. 'Chains' stretch out along the highways, where they supply food as efficiently and as swiftly as gas from a fuel pump. They also, by means of their repetitiveness, bind and homogenize city neighbourhoods. They supply in large measure modern man's apparent need to obliterate the difference between 'this place' and 'that', and to make as irrelevant as possible the distinction between 'now' and 'then'.

Uniformity, as every chain retailer is aware, makes good economic sense. Mass sales and ease of packaging and handling merchandise demand predictability – standard quality being, in the end, only one aspect of the sameness required. But the uniformity and the sheer volume of food supplied by fast-food chains are also expressions of our democratic aspirations. Everybody gets the same list of choices, everywhere. Nothing is served to which anyone could take exception, unless élitist notions, such as distaste for sweetness or demands for the personal touch, intrude. The aim is to please most people, and not to truckle to the difficult or pretentious few. The tastes of children are catered to especially. Grown-ups simply eat – and enjoy – what their children like. Abundant wrappings and boxes proclaim technologically perfected hygiene and simultaneously suggest a child's party 47 with presents. Taste blandness also flattens out differences among adults: there are no strong 'weird' flavours creating exclusive group preferences and societal distinctions.

Speed of service not only attacks the time limitation, it forestalls an increasingly widespread incapacity to be kept waiting, even if waiting might be a prerequisite for superior food. Speed also helps make certain that hierarchical formality cannot arise. Formality stratifies by organizing space and relationship, and to do this it takes time. It is true that we are 'served' from behind the counter, and that the preparation and 'further processing' which any single food item has undergone is achieved only through the expertise of an army of scientists and marketing agents and the toil of a host of machine operators – but we never see any of this. We witness only the swiftly and smartly performed final step as the food is handed to us, cartoned and wrapped, crumbed and sandwiched. There is no involvement with the personnel of the restaurant. Everything is impersonal; the very language used in ordering and serving may be pre-learned, almost ritualized. The method prevents time-wasting and possibly complex exchanges, and irrelevant chat. It is all so honed-down, rational, and predictable that it is difficult to imagine how we could further mechanize the process.

GALLUS GALLUS

In the forests of northern India, through Burma, Thailand, Kampuchea, and down to Sumatra, there lives a wild, shy, and easily angered bird. It is about one kilogram (2 lb) in weight when fully grown, with dark olive-to-bluish legs, a black breast, and shining reddish-brown back and tail feathers. It has a distinctive fleshy crest on its head, and an unnerving cackle and scream. *Gallus gallus*, the Red Jungle Fowl, was identified by Charles Darwin as the originator of the modern domestic chicken. Other jungle fowl are now thought to have contributed to the gene stock. But the Red Jungle Fowl, which is still abundant in its region of origin, looks very like a small and streamlined version of our own farm poultry.

It is commonly believed that domestication of the chicken occurred long after human beings had learned to tame and systematically exploit many other kinds of animals. This is because the shy jungle fowl would never have voluntarily associated itself with man or scavenged from him as did the other beasts we first learned to live with and to subjugate: animals like the dog, the goat, and the sheep. In fact, the earliest use of the cock for man appears to have been as a focus of religiously oriented sport. The people of the Indus Valley had domesticated the jungle fowl by 2000 BC. A seal from Mohenjo Daro, one of the Indus Valley's twin capital cities, depicts two cocks fighting.

Neither domestic fowl nor hens' eggs became fundamentally important in human diet until Roman times; indeed for half their recorded history, and in many places to this day, it has been the male of the species which was most valued – for cock-fighting, as a pet alarm clock, or as a provider of beautiful long tail feathers for sartorial adornment. The hens' eggs were eaten in small quantities by some and regarded as abominations by others. Actually eating chicken meat was usually thought barely worthwhile. The wild jungle fowl does not have a great deal of flesh on it, and once the aforementioned purposes of the domesticated chicken had

been served for long enough and the bird was killed,

it was tough, dry, and generally unrewarding. Meat-lovers, until recent times, could easily hunt flesh which was more delicious as well as more copious.

Throughout the countries of the jungle fowl's origin, and including the Pacific Islands, Tibet, and Mongolia, the chicken is thought to be a prophetic bird: divination by means of its bones, and sometimes through inspection of its intestines or liver, has been a matter of solemn human concern. Chicken bones have fine perforations in them which vary from fowl to fowl. Bamboo splinters are inserted into the holes and project at different angles; directions and distances between splinters are then measured and made the basis of chicken-bone divination. (The bones of intensively bred modern chickens exhibit far smaller variations in the number and position of the perforations; they make a much less satisfactory medium for magic than those of birds closer to the wild.)

Chicken divination has an intense following still among tribes in upper Burma and in Thailand, and a long history among the tribal populations of southern China. It is a fascinating fact that in Africa, where chickens spread sporadically (until a hundred years ago many tribes had never seen them, but others had cultivated them for centuries), divination by chicken blood and bones is also practised. Some African tribes keep cocks to wake them up in the morning, others keep them for their feathers. Others again use chickens in various sacrificial rituals. Many refuse on any account to eat chickens or their eggs, or both, and regard the birds as sacred messengers between us and the world beyond. These attitudes are extraordinarily similar to those held in south-east Asia and in ancient Iran. Following the trail of these customs, we can perhaps see how the Indian fowl reached and then travelled through Africa, via the chicken-divining regions of Ethiopia, the Sudan, and Uganda.

The reasons why Africans from many tribes refuse to eat chicken flesh, or deny it to sections of their societal groups, are various. Hens, for instance, may be considered promiscuous and careless about family structures ('they lay their eggs here and there'), and generally incapable of important distinctions ('they eat whatever they come across: worms, bugs, excrement, anything'). African women may therefore be warned against eating them, for fear of taking on the characteristics of what they consume. In much the same way chickens are thought unclean by high-caste Indian Hindus because the creatures show no discrimination in their eating habits: a Brahmin should take a purificatory bath after touching a chicken. Loathing of chicken serves also to distinguish Hindus from Moslems, who eat a great deal of poultry. Buddhists are nauseated by domestic fowl because they eat living worms and bugs; in Tibet, chickens are loathed for their claws which resemble those of the vultures which pick at corpses. Food always symbolically underpins societal categories; foods are often forbidden because they are perceived as violations of the system. It is not necessary to be consciously aware of a structural violation; one reacts simply and directly with avoidance and abhorrence.

Eggs, the world over, are symbols of fertility and of pure and undifferentiated power, of a force which is as yet unharnessed and undirected. In the nineteenth century a German explorer in Africa was murdered because he horrified his hosts by devouring unspeakable eggs. In Pakistan, south-east Asia, the Pacific Islands, and in parts of Africa (again that insistent and surprising similarity) eggs are often thought to be delicacies – provided that the inside has turned visibly and palpably into a chicken fetus: potentiality must have committed itself before it can be found delectable. Eggs, for women, are sexy and therefore dangerous, or fertility-replacing (eating them might fool her body into not producing offspring itself), and strictly forbidden. Eggs may be thought of as hens' excrement and rejected as unclean.

When the Aryans invaded northern India in the second millennium BC, they quickly learned to admire the jungle fowl and decided that it was sacred; by about 1000 BC they had forbidden the eating of its flesh. Meanwhile the Sumerians had come into contact with domestic fowl through their distant trade with the Indus Valley. Chickens, from 2000 BC onward, have been exceedingly useful on long sea voyages: they lay eggs on board, perpetuate themselves, and grow quickly to an edible size. The Chinese have cultivated chickens since the second millennium BC. They bred huge fowl with dark heavy bones, black skin, thickly feathered legs, pink combs, and almost no ability to fly. The first of these Cochin or Shanghai chickens to reach Britain arrived as a present for the royal family in 1835; they caused a sensation, with tens of thousands of people fighting to get a glimpse of them. The event started a century-long devotion to the hobby and business of breeding different varieties of chickens in Europe and America.

For a long time it was thought that the ancient Egyptians had no knowledge of the chicken until Hellenistic times. That idea was shattered in 1923, when a limestone sherd from 1350 BC was found in a tomb in the Valley of the Kings near Thebes. It bears a swiftly but confidently drawn cock. The Egyptians appear not to have been concerned thereafter with chickens in their art and writing, until their incubators became the wonder of the Mediterranean world a thousand years later. Maybe they kept a very few chickens for mere amusement. Perhaps cocks were associated with the sun-religion of Akhnaton, and exterminated after the death of Tutankhamen. (Akhnaton's Hymn to the Sun of the fourteenth century BC celebrates a chick breaking out of its shell; but we do not know whether the bird is of the species *Gallus gallus* or not.) What is certain is that for food the Egyptians, as their art abundantly shows us, raised quails, as well as ducks, geese, and other non-gallinaceous birds.

The Theban pot-sherd ruins a previously clear 55

and obvious picture of a Mediterranean world ignorant of chickens until Greeks encountered Persians. There are no chickens in the Old Testament, and none in Homer or Hesiod. An eighth century BC Assyrian cylinder seal does depict a cock-fight, but Assyria was next door to Iran. After the Persian Wars, Greek literature begins to abound in references to chickens (which the Greeks often called 'Persian birds'), and Greek art pours out representations of them on coins, sculpture, and pottery.

The Persians had been obsessed with chickens, and especially with cocks, from the moment they began to import domestic fowl from India. The two sacred animals in Zoroastrian religion were the dog and the cock. The dog guarded households and flocks; the cock had a special relationship with fire and light which made his cry a terror to darkness and evil. Persians, who so honoured the light of the sun that they prayed and ritually bathed themselves at every sunrise, never permitted themselves to be separated from the sacred power of the cock. The long-fingered yellow demon of sleep, Bashyacta, would overcome everything if it were not for the challenge he daily receives from the cock.

Chickens spread north from Persia as well as

west: they were taken up by the Scythians who adorned their coffins with images of cocks; they became favourites of the Celts, the Gauls, and the ancient Britons. When Julius Caesar arrived in Britain in the first century BC the natives were already breeding cocks and hens. 'They think it unlawful to feed upon hares, chickens or geese,' he wrote, 'yet they breed them up for their amusement and pleasures': once more we find the fowl being reared for sport and its flesh forbidden as food. Cocks' powerfully spurred leg-bones have been found at sites of the Roman period in Britain; they confirm that cock-fighting, for which Britain was to be famous many centuries later, had already become popular.

The Romans, adopting and perfecting the technology of the Hellenistic Greeks, raised domestic fowl for eating, and especially for their eggs. The Romans learned the science of incubation from the Greeks and the Egyptians, and from the Greeks they learned how to castrate cocks to produce fat capons. They kept capons, which they called 'half-males', *semimares*, in battery cages as they did dormice and other table delicacies, and they sometimes forbade killing chickens for meat, not as the result of a taboo but because their eggs were too valuable. Roman writers on agriculture devote long passages to the correct raising and care of fowl; descriptions of Roman dinner-parties include among the courses gargantuan quantities of chicken and eggs.

The Romans had their own version of chicken-divination, which they called *auspicium ex tripudiis*. They took the auspices by throwing chickenfeed to a flock of sacred fowls. If the birds ate so greedily that the grain fell to the ground from their beaks and rhythmically bounced (the *tripudium* was a triple-step in a warlike dance), then the battle would be won; if not, it should not be undertaken. On one famous occasion during the First Punic War an exasperated Roman admiral named P. Claudius Pulcher, who wanted badly to attack the Carthaginians even though the chickens refused their feed, seized the sacred fowl and threw them overboard. 'If they will not eat,' he cried, 'let them drink!' — and lost the battle.

Gallus is the Roman word for the bird; some have thought that the name refers to France, *Gallia*, which may have been one early introducer of chickens to the Italian peninsula, Greek Sicily being the other. It is much more likely, however, that *gallus* comes from the same root as the word 'poultry'. This root is the Hindu word *pil*, which becomes *pullus* and *gallus* (Latin), *pollo* (Italian), *poulet* (French), and *pullet* (English). Another widely used stem for words designating chickens is thought also to originate in India: it is *kuk*, Sanskrit *kukata*, Latin *cucurio*, *kuku* in many African languages, *Küchlein* (German), *coq* (French), *kieken* (Dutch), *cock* and *chicken* in English.

The Portuguese first landed in Brazil on April 22, 1500. Within thirty years of that date chickens were described as common in South America. The newcomers would probably have brought some chickens on board ship with them, since sailors usually did this, but a thirty-year period seems unprecedentedly short for the extensive spreading of knowledgeable acquaintance with an entirely new domestic creature. Was there some kind of indigenous South American Jungle Fowl? Did the indefatigable Polynesians, who undoubtedly got their chickens originally from Asia, carry the domestic fowl across the ocean long before the Europeans arrived?

The Indians of South America are described by the early European settlers as keeping their chickens for their feathers and for cock-fighting; they would seldom eat either the birds or their eggs. This behaviour did not follow European example, except for the pleasure in cock-fighting; indeed it seems strangely reminiscent of Asian practice, and of that of the African tribes who are believed to have received chickens ultimately from Asia. Another strange fact is that the last supreme Inca of Peru was named Atahualpa, and his uncle was called Hualpa. *Hualpa*, in the Quechua language, means 'chicken'. Did the Incas call chickens (newly arrived from Europe) after their ruler, or were the supreme Inca and his uncle named after chickens (already well known in Peru)?

There exists in South America today a race of chicken which looks very similar to certain Asiatic breeds. They are called Araucanas, after the Chilean Indian mountain tribe which raised them, and which had almost no contact with Europeans until the end of the nineteenth century. Pure-bred Araucanas are black-skinned and rumpless (lacking the final segments of the spinal column), with ear puffs, pea combs, and 'silky' or hair-like feathers; all of these are characteristics of Asian fowl rather than of European breeds. They also, uniquely in the poultry world, lay green and blue eggs. If the Polynesians brought chickens to South America from the east before the Europeans arrived, it means that the voyagers travelled fast, because chickens need water, and could not have survived a long, slow, drifting journey.

THE FIGHTING COCK

Ever since the first domestication of the jungle fowl, cocks have been raised and appreciated for a great deal more than their final fate in the family cooking pot. They were potent expressions of power and paradox, and symbols of masculine courage and prestige.

The domestic cock greets light with sound. This daily miracle has led him to be considered a sacred bird, a boundary marker, both link and distinction between sight and sound, light and dark, life and death, here and the beyond. The weird association of light with the cock's crow made him a chaser of darkness and, with that, of evil; he awoke men from the death of sleep and so symbolized the Messianic Age for Jews and the Resurrection for Christians.

The steeples of many churches are topped for this reason with the figure of a cock.

The crowing cock frightened away ghosts, as Horatio in *Hamlet* explains he has heard it said; and the fourth-century hymn of St Ambrose greets the singing dawn rooster who returns hope to the sick and to travellers, releases them from the fear of robbers, and restores faith to doubters. An Italian boy-child born with the crowing of the cock was often named Galeazzo, so that he would remember this lucky concurrence of events all his life. Among the Germans, the cock was associated in folklore and magic with fire; his comb in particular was symbolic of flames.

Gods associated with light loved the cock: Helios, Ahura Mazda, Mithras, and Osiris, to whom, in Hellenistic times, black or variegated cocks and white cocks were sacrificed, because he was a dying-and-rising god, one who knew both the underworld and the light of the sun. The cock has been called upon symbolically to participate in mysteries concerned with immortality. He was sacred to Asclepius, the Greek god of healing, whose mythology concerned dying and restoring to life. The philosopher Socrates asked on his deathbed for a cock to be sacrificed on his behalf in honour of Asclepius, for he believed he was not dying but recovering and awakening to a more abundant life. In Mohammedan legend, the Prophet saw in the First Heaven a vast cock whose crest brushed the boundary of the Second Heaven. It is the crowing of this cosmic fowl which awakens every living creature except man; and when it ceases to crow the Day of Judgement will be at hand.

A cooked cock, in several medieval stories, stood up and crowed in his dish, thereby revealing a crime which till then had remained hidden; a living hen and cock are still kept in memory of such a legend in a church on the pilgrimage route to Compostela in northern Spain. Sometimes people have avoided keeping cocks because of their crowing: the Kikuyu of Kenya because they did not want their whereabouts given away to their enemies or their victims, the ancient Greek Sybarites (allegedly) because they liked sleeping late in the mornings.

The magnificent cocks on the silver coins of Himera, a Greek city in Sicily, are puns on the city's name: *Himera* suggests both 'day' and 'sexual desire'. The cock has always been a byword for its lust – to the point where, in many languages besides

English, *cock* is synonymous with the male sexual organ itself. It was for this reason that in Victorian and especially in nineteenth-century North American usage the word *rooster* was substituted as the bird's name. Cocks' combs and cocks' testicles have seemed from time immemorial powerful aphrodisiacs. In ancient Greece a cock was a gift with specific sexual connotations from an older male to a young boy. The cock expressed the sheer maleness of the couple, their virile aggressivity and energy. (The alternative gift, a hare, referred to the joys of the chase: the boy's unwillingness and flight being considered to be as erotically enticing as a woman's 'playing hard to get'.)

Men have always found in the cock a model of pugnacity and courage. It is the bird's instinct to be easily aroused to rage, to fly at his opponent, and to fight till one or both of them drop dead; while a cock can crawl – no matter how battered and mutilated he is – he will fight on. The sight of cock facing cock has inspired men with battle-lust (the Greek general Themistocles was said to have roused his men to emulate fighting cocks), has urged them to fling themselves into competitive exploits (the goddess Athene appears together with a cock on vases won as prizes for athletic victories), and has encouraged them to strut in the panoplies of male pride. Does not the cock wear a crested 'helmet', spurs and plumes, and wattles which in many languages are known as 'beards'? The hubristic swagger of the cock has found its way into many English expressions. A *coxcomb* means an insolent upstart; a man may be as *cocky* as a rooster with crest erect and looking for trouble. The *cocksure* are bound someday to get what is coming to them, and when they do they must expect to be *crestfallen*.

Cock-fighting is thought by some to be the oldest living sport. The joy men took in watching cock-fights almost certainly led to the domestication of the bird in the first place; and the sacred status of cocks from earliest times must have meant that this sport, like so many others, was imbued in the beginning with religious significance. There is no doubt that cock-fighting even today is profoundly theatrical; the audience invest the combatants with symbolic roles, so that they act out the aggressions and struggles for power of the gamblers and betters standing (or rather, 'shouting, bawling, pounding, and vociferating like a very Babel') in a ring around the padded cockpit. The process can have a complex societal role, letting off emotional steam in a manner harmless to the spectators.

In the first century BC, cock-fights were held annually in the Athenian theatre sacred to the phallic, orgiastic, and gorgeously costumed god Dionysus; a cock-fight is carved on the marble throne of the god's priest, with the winged boy Agon, the personification of contest, setting the cocks ready to fight. In Aristophanes' comedy, *Clouds*, where 'Right' and 'Wrong' do battle with words, the two actors may well have been dressed as fighting cocks. An early use for the sport may have been as a decision-making device: an impossibly difficult choice found dramatic resolution through the impersonation by fighting cocks of the two possibilities, one being 'killed off' by the other. Cocks are equals and alike; from earliest times a fighting pair of them has been made to represent the relentless savagery of civil war. The cocks' wounds and death may on occasion have constituted a kind of ritual scapegoats' sacrifice to avert man's own violence and prevent it from destroying his society. In any event, it was commonly felt that a cock-fight was not only simple fun to watch, but also a drama with several messages, and that the lessons needed to be drawn, witnessed, and endlessly repeated.

Cocks, like men, are armed for battle with lethal metal swords. The cock's natural spurs are removed from its legs and on to the stumps are bound one of two kinds of metal spur: sword-like slashing blades are traditional in the East, and sharp points in the West. The method helps to equalize the combatants since natural spurs vary a good deal in length and strength. The metal weapons are designed to draw blood and so increase the excitement, and, in fact, a single blow from one of these weapons often kills. 'Naked-heel' fighting, with natural spurs and no metal weapons, is preferred in India and in some other Eastern countries; in this form of the sport endurance is valued more highly than speed or agility. A naked-heel fight can last a whole day. This devotion to taking one's time over one's pleasures is completely different from the typical Western enjoyment of short and violent sensations, timed by the stop-watch. Cocks in some places are 'dubbed' before a fight: their wattles and crest are cut off, much as a soldier used to remove his beard before battle in case an enemy snatched and held it. The birds may wear hoods into the fray, like fighting airplane pilots.

Before the fight, cocks live a glorious life. They are massaged, exercised, petted, and admired: bathed, shampooed, and fed on delicacies. Exercising one's rooster meant jogging behind him to keep him running, and every now and then presenting him with an ordinary cock (which had to be carried under the owner's arm for protection) to encourage his irritability and aggression. In ancient Greece and Egypt, garlic or bread sopped in wine was considered especially fortifying for cocks; South Americans like to give them hot chili-peppers; in eighteenth-century England we hear of them being given pastries made of wheaten flour, eggs, and large quantities of butter. An owner had personally to find and supply the varieties of living grubs and insects which his game cock particularly fancied. A man 'fed like a fighting cock' was uncommonly sleek.

The master of a cock, in many societies, has been found to identify himself, and especially his sexual prowess, closely with his bird. Clifford Geertz, the anthropologist, can describe fighting cocks as being for the Balinese 'ambulant genitals with a life of their own'. In ancient Greek art the cock was often made explicitly to resemble a male's sexual organs. All kinds of more or less overt sexual symbolism surrounds the care given to cocks before and during the fight. They are caressed, fed sexually stimulating food, ceremonially bathed in scented water or in urine. During the fight, a bleeding cock has its wounds licked by his master – who might be moved actually to put the chicken's whole head into his mouth, sucking and blowing, in order to revive it. The method is used all over the world, although it is often considered a rather affected gesture. Spurs may be dramatically licked before the fight begins, to prove that they have not been poisoned. Cock-fighting is like wrestling: a celebration of rampant virility, with melodramatic flourishes, extravagant displays of resolution, honour, arrogance, and excess, huge stylized gestures, and a violent climax where inseparably interwoven Chance and Design are seen irresistibly to have taken effect.

Men from widely different social backgrounds have always met and mixed at cock-fighting bouts. It seems clear that the discovery of a common base-line fellowship among lords, workers, peasants, and bourgeois males is part of the essence of the exercise.

The outlawing of cock-fighting, which began to be effected in England in 1834, was a symptom of deep-seated changes in society. A general increase in social equality would reduce society's need dramatically to express the natural similarity among men in a system where class rules were rigid and waived only on special occasions. There would be less flaunting of bloodlust from then on; cruelty was to take a new, less colourful and individualistic, more concealed and more efficient turn, as human beings conceived and perfected factory farming.

Yet the ancient sport lives on. It is widespread in South and Central America and in the Caribbean countries, and it also exists in spite of the non-violence of religions like Buddhism and Hinduism in India and south-east Asia, the lands where the birds originated. Today the Philippine Islands are probably the world centre for cocking; international 'mains' (large cock-fighting contests) take place there from time to time. In the United States and Europe, where it is forbidden by law, cock-fighting continues to flourish illegally. All the traditions, the lore, the breeds, and the intricate rules are maintained and handed on, a furtive survival of an ancient passion in a world which, officially at least, has little room and less sympathy for strutting and flamboyant masculinity or for violence accorded gaudy enjoyment and studied respect.

MOTHER HEN

Light rouses the cock to crow, and it is light which passes through the hen's eye, activates the pituitary gland at the base of her skull to secrete certain hormones in her body, and starts her ovary working to lay eggs. Every baby hen hatches with five or six thousand microscopic egg-germs already awaiting completion in her body. She is ready to begin creating and laying from this vast store when she is about six months old.

The hen's ovary is a very large organ, because although she is a big bird, her eggs are enormous in relation to her body size – they are so big that she can carry only one egg to completion in her body at a time. Hens, like all female vertebrates, begin with paired ovaries; but in her case the right ovary withers away so that only one egg needs to be given space. Only a tiny fraction of the egg-germs she carries will eventually end up as eggs; what it is that makes these privileged few do so is unknown. Quite naturally, scientists would dearly like to understand and then draw profit from knowledge of the mechanism.

The female hormone estrogen is partly responsible for the hen's behaviour both in making her submissive to the cock at coition, and in causing her to seek and prepare a nest in which to lay her eggs. It apparently even causes her to emit a pre-laying call. Nest-preparation is so biologically necessary as part of the laying process that caged battery hens will often cry out and struggle to obey this part of nature's demand.

Hens lay according to the length of daylight; when days are short (in winter when it is too cold to raise chicks) there is not enough light, under natural conditions, to rouse the hen's ovary to mature eggs within her body. Once light has triggered intense hormonal activity in the hen, ovulation occurs about six or eight hours later. She will now begin laying eggs, usually one every twenty-five hours. In ovulation, the yolk erupts from the ovary's constraining membranes and is drawn down the oviduct into the hen's infundibulum. At this point the yolk rests for fifteen minutes in its journey, and it is during this pause that fertilization may occur, whether directly or by male sperm stored in the hen's body. After these fifteen minutes the yolk will move on and then begin to be surrounded by white, by its two membranes, and by the shell: sperm penetration is rendered impossible. It is a common misapprehension that fertilization is required for an egg to be produced; this is not the case. The vast majority of hens' eggs are now marketed unfertilized so that they will not develop into chicks. Even the presence of a minute blood spot such as occurs in fertilized eggs (without harming them nutritionally in any way), revolts many people in our culture, and such eggs are not kosher in the Jewish tradition. A tiny haemorrhage sometimes occurs at ovulation, producing a little blood on the surface of the yolk, again harmlessly.

The yolk is moved from the hen's infundibulum, again by muscular contractions, into the magnum, where it rotates and is swathed in egg white, which twists at the long ends like a candy wrapper: the white's end-knots are easily found when an egg is cracked open. The membranes are added during the hour the egg takes to pass down the isthmus of the oviduct; the two membranes are in contact with 73 each other over the whole surface of the egg white, except at the egg's blunt end, where they part company to form the air sac. In the uterus or shell gland the egg waits eighteen to twenty hours as calcium salts from the tissue of this cavity create the shell, and the hen's body gently kneads the egg into its oval (literally, 'eggy') shape. Again, what it is that prompts the hen to lay her egg is not completely understood. The act takes only a few seconds and it is often greeted by the hen with a cackle of triumph.

When she has laid a number of eggs, another hormonal change takes place in her body. One of the hormones involved is prolactin, a substance named after its effect in mammals, which is to make the female breast produce milk. It causes instinctual maternal behaviour in all vertebrate creatures: amphibians return to water in order to lay eggs, the female fowl anxiously gathers her chicks together when night falls. Prolactin also makes hens 'broody', that is, intent upon sitting on the eggs they have laid and keeping them warm till they hatch. (Broodiness is a thorough nuisance in battery or factory layers: one reason for the preference for

White Leghorns over all others in factory farming

is that, with the help of careful breeding, they are chickens lacking an intense brooding instinct.)

A broody hen fluffs up her feathers until she is almost twice her normal size. Her tail feathers rise and spread. She stays that way all through brooding, hatching, and raising her young. The reason for the physical change is that with these feathers she keeps her eggs warm, and also finds room under them for the hatched chicks. As soon as her chicks are ready for independence, the hen's feathers subside, she suddenly and totally ignores her offspring, and they just as unconcernedly abandon her. Part of this transformation is due to the subsidence of the hen's feathers: the chicks have known her by her ballooning size and shape, by her maternal clucks, and her general motherly concern. Her diminished size as her feathers lie down, and her loss of the mothering urge, combine to make her simply unrecognizable to her chickens – and out of sight is out of mind. So nature, at precisely the right moment, painlessly severs the close and vital tie between mother and babies.

During the three weeks it takes a hen to hatch her eggs, her temperature rises and she needs very little to eat. She sits tight on the nest and refuses to move, except for about fifteen minutes a day when she rushes off to grab enough food and drink for survival, before hurrying back to her duty. (So closely calculated is nature's provision for the welfare of hen and eggs that artificial incubators have regularly to be cooled for fifteen minutes to allow for this rest-period in a hen's day.) Three times daily the hen must turn every egg in her nest with her beak, in order to ensure that they are warmed all over, and to prevent the embryos inside from sticking to the shells.

Although the eggs were laid over a period of up to three weeks before the hen began to brood over them, all the chicks hatch, after an incubation period of approximately twenty-one days, within forty-eight hours of each other. Forty-eight hours is the amount of time a hen can stay on her nest without leaving and the length of time a chick just out of its shell can survive without food or water. (The latter fact is of enormous importance for modern hatcheries, which use the bonus in time for the transport of baby chicks from incubating firms to fatteners.) The first-born chick begins peeping in its shell twenty-four hours before it hatches; the

others soon take up the cry, thus notifying each

other and their mother that zero-hour is approaching. Experiments with turkeys have shown that a chick's cheeping is a matter of life and death to it. If a mother turkey hears no sound from her nestling (the experimenters deafened a turkey hen to see what would happen), she immediately pecks it to death, taking it for a nest enemy. In a turkey's brain the sight of a chick is not enough; the sound must complete the picture.

When its time comes, the chick saws its way out of the shell with a rough piece of its bill which is called an 'egg tooth'; this specialized piece of anatomy disappears after use. The mother hen has to concentrate as, one by one, underneath her and out of her sight, the chicks struggle out of their shells and lie down, exhausted and faintly cheeping, to recover from their ordeal. One false move and the hen may trample some of her brood to death, or smother them. Once the chick's down is dry, it begins peeping loudly, largely to help the mother know where it is. The muffled cheeps in the shells also keep her informed of how much longer she needs to stay on the nest.

When the whole brood is hatched, the hen sallies forth with her chickens, who are ready immediately to feed themselves. What they continue to need is their mother's warmth and it is again through their cheeps that the chicks let her know their need. The hen will suddenly (without any warning discernible to us) squat down on the ground, and the chicks will rush under her outspread wings and feathers and stay there until they are warmed through, after which they will set off again on their perpetually exciting quest for bugs, grubs, and seeds.

MAN'S EYE VIEW

In spite of the fact that chickens have seldom roused people's affections – they are too scratchy, self-absorbed, un-mammalian, and, above all, too edible for that – the cock, the hen, and their chicks have always lived close to their owners' houses. They need protection, especially at night, from the predators which are constantly after their eggs and their flesh; they are kept close by for feeding purposes; and their nests need constantly to be checked for their contents. The care of barnyard animals – rabbits, chickens, ducks, and the rest – has always been women's work, 'house' work, along with everything concerned with milk and dairying. Constantly under the eye of their human owners, chickens have been in all societies the subjects of speculation, moralizing, fable-telling, and mythologizing.

Cocks have always delighted us with their pride, their dignified and angry flamboyance, their sexual vigour, and their courage. A cock may almost achieve the status of a pet, not only because of his useful crow, but also because he is perceived as the walking achievement of a swaggering and self-confident *macho* ideal. We have already remarked that men may see cocks as actually embodying their own sexual prowess, and allow the sight of a bloody cock-fight to spur them to battle.

The Greek god Hermes had a great deal in common with cocks. Similarities include his winged, intensely masculine and phallic nature; his role as psychopomp or leader of the souls across the boundary separating life from death; and his patronage of eloquence. The cock crows, and people listen: this was conclusive proof that public eloquence was a quintessentially male virtue. The hen's modest cluck showed that women should keep their words short and low, and attuned to domestic concerns. The rooster was thought to symbolize the church preacher, warning and rousing his flock; it followed that holding forth, in women and hens, was inappropriate and ridiculous. The cock 'rules the roost', and protects his womenfolk from other cocks and from foreign marauders. His manner of 'possessing' a hen sexually is violent and imperious; she simply, silently, and apparently without pleasure, submits. The cock has provided a richly suggestive model for the maintenance of masculine prestige. It was not a model meant to be a Christian ideal, however. The only time chickens get into the New Testament, aside from the dawn crow of the cock when Peter had denied knowing Jesus three times, is when Jesus compared himself not to a rooster but to a mother hen, longing to gather the children of Jerusalem like chickens under his wings.

Barnyard fowl (not game-cocks and their cock-breeding spouses, whose symbolism is entirely different) have in our own culture, and until our own day, been thought the easiest of creatures to feed. There was nothing 'scientific' about it; hens foraged for food and were grateful for scraps. People marvelled at how generously productive the homely and easily pleased hen could be. (In different cultures, the hen, as mentioned earlier, is an abomination precisely because she eats anything: her behaviour denotes promiscuity and lack of discrimination in the female, whose role is to embody the idea of purity itself.)

Chickens have one of the toughest digestive tracts on earth; if they habitually eat hard objects they solve the problem simply by swallowing stones which lodge in their gizzards and help in the grinding process. The 'corn cycle', which used to operate on many American farms, began with the feeding of whole kernels to cattle. Unchewed corn passed through the cows and into their excrement. Hogs scavenged in the dung, and ate the corn they found in it; sharp-eyed chickens were then allowed to hunt through the pigs' manure for particles of undigested corn. European visitors were amazed at American ingenuity and at the saving of waste and labour. There was no grinding of corn and no need for feed containers. The hen took refuse and turned it into gold. She was a modest, hard-working, and submissive wife, as irreproachably fecund and maternally devoted as she was thrifty. She was a model for nineteenth-century Protestant womanhood.

Her mate the cock (or rather, rooster) was a gentleman, and punctual with his crowing. He looked after his family; it was his duty, because he was stronger and cleverer than they, to show them where they could find food, and people often claimed they had witnessed his fatherly concern. Because he was a bird he could afford openly to have many wives whereas a modicum of discretion was required when a Victorian gentleman kept mistresses or pursued his female servants. The cock made quite certain, of course, that he alone was in charge of his household by keeping upstart roosters fiercely at bay. His womenfolk could be very difficult at times – but he kept them in order through his patience and his effortless masculine prestige. 'It belongs to their very nature,' wrote a nineteenth-century authority on hens, 'to be marshalled by one of the stronger sex, who is a kind, though a strict master, and a considerate, though stern disciplinarian.'

In 1922, a Norwegian psychologist called T. Schjelderup-Ebbe officially demonstrated that hens themselves observed what he called a 'pecking order'. One hen dominates the rest and demands signs of submission, in particular a cowering demeanour and lowered head; she pecks any insufficiently humble hen into subordination. The hens lower in prestige than herself similarly browbeat others, and so on down until one poor creature is constantly set upon by the rest, being pecked by all the others and having no one herself to peck. Especially fierce battles result if newcomers are introduced into an established order. Cocks easily rule over all hens; it is a very sorry specimen of rooster that allows himself to be 'hen-pecked'.

The discovery of the pecking order in chickens was received less as a revelation than as confirmation of what everyone knew to be the case. Some chickens (and people, of course) are better and stronger than others; it is sensible – and it was now 'proved' to be natural as well – to reinforce this state of affairs with any means at our disposal. It was considered especially fascinating to discover that women (that is, hens) are guilty of this behaviour among themselves, with the extremely poignant proviso that any male could impose his authority over his womenfolk at any time. Fewer reflections have been inspired by the fact that pecking order develops only when chickens are kept in confinement; the fierce territorial instinct of the birds, ensuring as it does that each family has enough land on which to feed, has positive value 83 and less violent effects when they live uncaged.

Sex roles, after all, had been confirmed by chickendom since ancient times. Aelian tells us that cocks were kept in the temple of Herakles, while his wife Hebe had hens. Between the temple flowed 'a never-failing channel of clear water'. Hens absolutely never went into the temple of Herakles, whereas cocks at mating time flew over the stream to choose their mates. When, after fertilizing the hens, they returned to their home, they were 'cleansed by the water that separates the sexes'. A cock sometimes helps a hen to hatch eggs, Aelian avers elsewhere, and when he does so he ceases to be able to crow: 'I fancy he is conscious that he is then doing the work of a female and not of a male.'

When a hen produced a small malformed egg, as happens sometimes at a first laying, the unsuccessful object used to be called a 'cock's egg' or 'cokeney' in early English. The word was often used of a foolish or spoilt child, the pride of its doting mother; and then by country people to put down soft and ignorant city-dwellers. The expression was taken over by Londoners and used with pride: it is the origin of the name *Cockney*.

A hen sometimes develops spurs, a masculine

trait. Such a bird has always been destined for the pot, or at any rate for death, because people believed she could not be a good layer and in any case was liable to pierce any eggs she produced with her spurs. It is a fact which cannot escape the notice of even the most unwilling witness that hens quite often crow. Such an event has always been considered sinister – an omen of war, of a death in the family, of a breakdown in society. The separation of male and female roles has until recently formed the basis of societal structure, to the extent that any tampering with the categories suggested the collapse of order. Cocks and hens had to conform to the roles we projected on to them, and to confirm for us the moulds we forced upon each other.

'The barnyard rooster,' according to a recent history of European and American food economics, 'is now a figment of the urbanite's imagination.' As increasing equality between men and women gives us entirely new spectacles through which to view the social scene, the cock and his mate automatically lose their secondary and literary use as an Aesopian representation of our sexual roles and a proof of wisdom in our organization of human relationships. At almost the same moment, the whole flock of 85 barnyard fowl has disappeared from our view, to be locked away, forced to conform to a utilitarian scheme, deprived of as many of their natural behavioral patterns as are thought inconvenient, and pressured ever more relentlessly to produce. Let us hope that the suspicion does not become even more insistent that once again we might be thrusting upon chickens a role which is a kind of prophetic model, a metaphor for the general direction of present human goals, and for the price we are prepared to pay, and to make others pay, in order to satisfy what we perceive to be our needs.

PENGUIN 60s

PENGUIN 60s

READ MORE IN PENGUIN

For complete information about books available from Penguin and how to order them, please write to us at the appropriate address below. Please note that for copyright reasons the selection of books varies from country to country.

IN THE UNITED KINGDOM: Please write to *Dept. EP, Penguin Books Ltd, Bath Road, Harmondsworth, Middlesex UB7 0DA.*

IN THE UNITED STATES: Please write to *Consumer Sales, Penguin USA, P.O. Box 999, Dept. 17109, Bergenfield, New Jersey 07621-0120.* VISA and MasterCard holders call 1-800-253-6476 to order Penguin titles.

IN CANADA: Please write to *Penguin Books Canada Ltd, 10 Alcorn Avenue, Suite 300, Toronto, Ontario M4V 3B2.*

IN AUSTRALIA: Please write to *Penguin Books Australia Ltd, P.O. Box 257, Ringwood, Victoria 3134.*

IN NEW ZEALAND: Please write to *Penguin Books (NZ) Ltd, Private Bag 102902, North Shore Mail Centre, Auckland 10.*

IN INDIA: Please write to *Penguin Books India Pvt Ltd, 706 Eros Apartments, 56 Nehru Place, New Delhi 110 019.*

IN THE NETHERLANDS: Please write to *Penguin Books Netherlands bv, Postbus 3507, NL-1001 AH Amsterdam.*

IN GERMANY: Please write to *Penguin Books Deutschland GmbH, Metzlerstrasse 26, 60594 Frankfurt am Main.*

IN SPAIN: Please write to *Penguin Books S. A., Bravo Murillo 19, 1° B, 28015 Madrid.*

IN ITALY: Please write to *Penguin Italia s.r.l., Via Felice Casati 20, I-20124 Milano.*

IN FRANCE: Please write to *Penguin France S. A., 17 rue Lejeune, F-31000 Toulouse.*

IN JAPAN: Please write to *Penguin Books Japan, Ishikiribashi Building, 2-5-4, Suido, Bunkyo-ku, Tokyo 112.*

IN GREECE: Please write to *Penguin Hellas Ltd, Dimocritou 3, GR-106 71 Athens.*

IN SOUTH AFRICA: Please write to *Longman Penguin Southern Africa (Pty) Ltd, Private Bag X08, Bertsham 2013.*